APPLY HBCU

TRAVIS A. RICHARD

Dedicated to my nieces and nephews, never stop soaring.

And to my beloved HBCU, thank you.

A special thank you and dedication to my mother who gained her wings on April 16, 2021. Your love, knowledge, and wisdom have been instrumental to my growth. I'll forever cherish our moments and tools you've provided for success. I love you and miss you Momma.

TABLE OF CONTENTS

Foreword

I am pleased to write this foreword, not only because Travis Richard has been my best friend for over 17 years but also because of the message in this book. *Apply HBCU* unfolds a fantastic story about a small-town kid whose life was destined, despite his struggles, to introduce him to people and places that would help, heal and harvest the extreme amount of potential energy that yearned to be activated.

Living only a quarter of a mile from each other, growing up, we hung out all the time. We were both band geeks and loved music. From high school through college, it was pretty much our lives. With my dad being the high school band director, we had unlimited access to the band room. If he had agreed to bring us a sandwich and a few snacks, a small ask, we probably would never have left. Unfortunately, our parents insisted that there was life outside of the band room. Who knew?

What we didn't realize then was how the love of music would change our lives. Music was the catalyst to our professional development, and it was the lynchpin of our excitement to attend Southern University A&M College and march in the Human Jukebox Marching Band. Music taught us to structure, discipline and instilled the most unrelenting work ethic in us. Most importantly, it taught us how to work together for a common goal and objective harmony.

It is rare and humbling to have made it through some of the obstacles that life has thrown our way. It is rewarding to share testimonies of triumph and help those following our footsteps to navigate those same hurdles.

Travis' story shows us that one can be misguided yet find his or her way; one can deal with an abundance of misfortune but not be defeated, and one can be misinformed, however, seek knowledge. *Apply HBCU* is simply a story about what happens when preparation meets opportunity.

Remember, always be prepared because your opportunity is coming, and Travis is giving you the roadmap to get there.

Aaron Ventress
Southern University and A&M College, '10

Foreword

As a mother, I could not ask for a better son. I still remember the day T.J. came home and told me he had joined the marching band. At first, I didn't take him too seriously and said, "Yeah, okay." But he insisted he was serious. Not long after that conversation, I saw him perform for the first time, and it brought tears to my eyes. I was amazed! There was my T.J. shining like the star mama always knew he was.

We lived in a rough area where there were drugs, so I worried about him. He didn't hang around the wrong crew and never got into any trouble, but as a single parent, you have to think, "what if." He had a bit of a temper that he eventually outgrew, but overall he was a sweet kid. I would see other women who didn't care about their sons, but I cared about my boy, and I promised myself I would never let the streets have him.

Everyone raises their kids differently. I was a single mother who had gotten pregnant at 14 and had my first child at 15, so I was a little more lenient with my children. Growing up, my mom didn't allow us to have an opinion or thoughts as kids. Don't get me wrong, my children had rules, and they knew how far to go and not to be out in the streets or anything, but they also knew that if they failed, they could never say it was because their mama held them back.

T.J. was a perfectionist, so when he failed the 7th grade, I didn't fuss. I told him it was okay and that when you fall it's about getting up, and that as far as I was concerned, there was no way he was going to quit school as long as he was living in my home. I told him to do what he needed to do, and he did.

T.J. completely turned it around and was the first one in our immediate family to go to college. He set an example and stuck it out at Southern University. I didn't go to college, but I am proud that my son did. To this day, everywhere I go, I tell people my son graduated from Southern University.

I raised my son, but Southern University played a massive role in making him the man he is today. His peers and family respect him, and now he's writing a book to help young people navigate their way through college. It takes hard work and sacrifice to make it, but T.J. proves it can be done. I hope that you are encouraged and motivated by his story to *Apply HBCU*.

Phyllis Richard
Proud mother of an HBCU graduate

Message From The Author

It brings me immense joy and pleasure to present a story that changed the trajectory of my life. I cannot help but evoke the excitement, opportunities, and success that alumni of Historically Black Colleges and Universities (HBCUs) are continuing to represent. This moment takes me back to when America elected its first Black President, Barack Obama. November 4, 2008, was one of the most memorable moments of my undergraduate college experience. It was the first time I cast a ballot for the presidential election. On the Southern University and A&M College campus, the *circle* was filled with an elevated level of anxiousness. This feeling would later turn to joy, happiness, faith, belief, and courage. We witnessed a man of integrity and strength who looked like us and became the first Black President of the United States of America. Although he is not an alumnus of an HBCU , President Obama gave me that extra boost of confidence I needed as a Black, male college student. His election reassured me that I could conquer the world and anything I set my mind to do.

Twelve years later and I am now navigating my doctoral journey. It has not been easy, but it has been necessary. In addition to the journey of becoming Dr. Travis Richard, it has been six-years to completion of *Apply HBCU*. I have been delayed but not denied. Today is a true testament that God's timing is perfect. Witnessing Kamala Harris, a graduate of Howard University, an HBCU, elected as the first Black female Vice President of the United States is encouraging.

As I continue to embark on this journey to be the vision, hope, and change for higher education, I know that HBCU alumni continue to pave the way for young change agents like myself. I hope you enjoy learning how my HBCU prepared me to overcome obstacles, learn humility, and have grit. Remember, there is an HBCU for everyone, including you. *Apply HBCU.*

Notable HBCU Alumni: Stacy Abrams, Spelman College; Reverend Dr. Raphael Warnock, Morehouse College; Gregory Route, Sr., Grambling State University; Mayor Keisha Lance Bottoms; Florida A&M University; State Representative Edward "Ted" James, Southern University and A&M College.

CHAPTER 1

Born And Raised

"You never know what the future brings."
– Randy Jackson
Southern University and A&M College '79

My name is Travis Anthony Richard, and I was born and raised in Opelousas, a small city in Southwest Louisiana. Opelousas is one of those cities where practically everybody knows everybody, and all your family members live less than ten minutes away from one another. Opelousas is so small if you drive 20 minutes down I-90 in either direction, you've pretty much left it.

Though the city is small, it's home, and it's where I got my roots. It's also where my parents were born and raised, and as far as I know, it's where their parents were born and raised. My parents went to the same high school I would later graduate from, Opelousas Senior High. It's this same high school where they would eventually meet and become high school sweethearts.

My mom was a sophomore, and my dad was a graduating senior with aspirations of playing college football when my oldest sister was born. Three years later, in April of '87, I came along – a brown skin baby boy with my mom's stubbornness and the quick wit and bluntness of my dad. While my mom and her family were happy to welcome a new bundle of joy, my dad's parents weren't so pleased. They had dreams for my dad too, and somehow, they felt the births of my sister and me, more so me, had dashed those plans.

By the time I was born, my parents' relationship was rocky. Maybe it was because they were still so young, or perhaps it was because my father struggled with inner challenges. Whatever it was, it greatly affected me. I rarely saw my father and could count on one hand the number of times I spent any time with him.

My parents had an on-again, off-again relationship. I guess during one of their periods of being off, my mom and her best friend, my godmother Sherry, packed my sister and me up and moved us all to Charlotte, North Carolina. What began as a short vacation turned into my mom and godmother deciding to relocate. They were both in search of better opportunities than Opelousas could provide, and at the invitation of the family who already lived there, they decided to stay. Even though I was young at the time, I still have happy memories of living in Charlotte and riding around in my mom's silver Isuzu. We lived there for a short while before moving back to Opelousas to stay with my maternal grandmother, Irma Jean.

I loved living with Grandma Irma, and I was her favorite grandchild; I'm pretty sure my siblings and cousins would agree with me, lol. I could do no wrong in the eyes of Grandma Irma. I went everywhere with her and fondly remembered sitting out on the steps just talking and eating bananas, drinking Cokes, and reading the newspaper. For whatever reason, she liked calling me T. J. Hooker. For the longest time, I never knew why, until recently. T. J. Hooker was the name of one of Grandma Irma's favorite television shows and also the name of the main character, a no-nonsense police officer. My guess is my super stern personality and a knack for being a regulator who kept everyone in line reminded her of this show and her favorite character. I wasn't the oldest grandchild, but I carried myself like I was and treated everyone accordingly. I wore the nickname she gave me proudly. I loved me some Grandma Irma! We were thick as thieves, and no matter what happened, she would look out for me and defend me like none other.

Grandma Irma was a jazzy woman who wore fancy hats, lots of jewelry, and drove a maroon convertible with a white top. One time at Christmas, my paternal grandparents bought my sister and me some pajamas. It seemed like a nice gesture on the surface, but the problem came when my younger sister realized that all of the other grandkids had gotten pajama sets with cartoon characters, while the ones we got were plain. I was too young to put my finger on it, but I knew something wasn't right. I remember leaving my grandparents house and walking with my younger sister over to Grandma Irma's. After telling Grandma Irma what happened, she got agitated, loaded my sister and me into the car, and drove over to my other grandparents' house. We stayed in the car the entire time, but from what I could see they exchanged words before Grandma Irma returned to the car and sped away. A few days later, Grandma Irma bought my sister and me some cartoon themed pajamas. She was always thoughtful like that, and always looked out for me and made sure I was okay. She was my best friend. We lived with Grandma Irma until my mom found a new place right down the street from her.

I don't recall the exact moment it happened, but by the time we moved into our new house, my dad had started coming around again. It was never consistent. One day he'd be there in the house with us, and the next day he'd be gone. We never spent any holidays together and didn't take any family vacations. The only thing I remember about those times was the fights he and my mom would have. They were always fighting, both physical and verbal. It was traumatic, but it was normal for us. I guess my mom eventually got tired of him because he stopped coming around as much. He no longer lived with us, and though he lived less than ten minutes away, his presence in my life was limited. I don't recall ever doing anything with him, and he never came to any of my student events. Once my mom and dad split for good, the only time I remember seeing him was when I got in trouble at school and needed disciplining; this is when my love for him had begun to fade.

Rest in honor to my dad, Travis "Tra Dog" Stevens, and my maternal grandmother, Irma Jean Richard.

CHAPTER 2

F Sharp

"Failure is just another way to learn how to do something right."
– Marian Wright Edelman
Spelman College '60

For most of my early years, I did well in school. I remember getting awards, including those free pizza prizes they would give you for reading books. I was a good student, but by the time I got to fourth grade, I acted out more, or as my dad liked to call it, I was the class clown. I was young, ambitious, and misguided. Looking back at it, I was crying out for attention.

My mom was a single mother who worked a lot, which meant I had a lot of unsupervised time to get into trouble. I didn't get into any problems as far as [a lot of] fights and gangs go, but I was in my little world, doing my own thing and no longer applying myself in the classroom. My family didn't preach education, and there were no real expectations other than being an okay student. Because my mom was always working, I could get away with skipping school, and no one would ever know or question me about it. I did not have the family structure like those I'd seen when watching shows on T.V. like The Cosby Show or A Different World, so if I didn't want to study for tests or do homework, I didn't. Plus, I had a hard time understanding classwork. My mom once told me that my childhood doctor wanted to prescribe me medications for attention span and behavior, but Grandma Irma gave him a stern "Hell no!" Prescribing medicines for attention and behavior challenges and labeling students as special needs in low-income areas is common. If it's done "right," both the school and parent could receive monetary government assistance for the student. I know, it's terrible! After school, when other kids were doing homework, studying, and then getting ready for bed, I'd be out with my cousins riding bikes or playing video games. By the time I got in, it would be 9 or 10 P.M., so I'd spend the next morning debating with myself as to whether or not I wanted to go to school.

Unlike grammar school, where most of my teachers had been grade school friends of my mom, which meant I could reasonably get away with some things, my middle school teachers were not as gracious. By the time I got to 7th grade, all those days of never going home with a book had caught up with me – my failure to make school a priority had led to me failing the 7th grade. I was so embarrassed. How could

"Mr. Popular" have to repeat a grade? What would my friends think? The funny thing is my oldest sister had also failed 7th grade, so in some ways, I felt like it was a curse. The truth is it wasn't. I had failed because I was unable to do what was required and apply myself.

There were only two middle schools in Opelousas, and I remember begging my mom to let me go to summer school, so I wouldn't have to face the embarrassment of repeating a grade. She refused and said, "If you couldn't get it in ten months, you won't get it in two."

I was upset, but what could I do? I returned the following school year to the same school and the same grade. None of my friends knew I had failed, and I planned to keep it that way. Everything was going according to plan until a classmate playfully pulled my student I.D., which I intentionally wore backward so no one would see that it said 7th grade instead of eighth, and blurted out, "Travis, you're still in the 7th grade!" I was so hurt. Now everyone knew. You would think the embarrassment would be enough for me to get my act together, but it wasn't. I failed the 7th grade again. Yes, I failed twice, but because of a new school board policy and the recommendations of my teachers, I was able to pass to the eighth grade anyway. "Whew, chile!" I had passed by the seat of my pants. Something about failing this time and only being promoted because of a change to the policy didn't sit well.

"Don't feel entitled to anything you didn't sweat and struggle for."
– Marian Wright Edelman
Spelman College '60

I knew I needed to get it together, so I began adjusting my mindset and how I approached academics. It was a slow start, but the shift was starting to take root; this was the start of me realizing that I never wanted things to be given to me because I did not value them as much as if I earned them.

"Both tears and sweat are salty, but they render a different result. Tears will get you sympathy; sweat will get you change."
– Jesse Jackson
North Carolina A&T State University '64

At the start of my 8th grade year, I knew I needed to take an elective, and because I had already taken P.E. twice, I decided to take band, an elective that only 8th graders could take. I had never played an instrument in my life, but I had older cousins in the high school marching band, and I loved hearing them play. The band director, Mr. Leroy Ventress, started me off as a percussionist, snare drum, to be more specific. I wish I could say I was good, but I wasn't. I sucked, like terrible. I quickly went from playing the drums to playing the tuba, and that, surprisingly, is where I excelled. I was good at band fundamentals, so Mr. Ventress took notice and began encouraging me. As a kid who didn't get much attention, I rallied around his feedback. In one breath, he'd compliment me on my skills and talent to the applause of the entire class, and in the next, he'd school me on my need to find balance and apply myself in the classroom. He'd always tell me, "Regardless of your gifts and talents, you won't make it far if you don't learn to master being a student musician." Eventually, this would begin to make sense to me.

Mr. Ventress was like a father to me. His youngest son, Aaron, who was in the same grade as me, would later become my best friend. Meeting the two of them forever changed the path of my life. I had been friends with Aaron since 8th grade, and unlike me, he comes from a two-parent household where both of his parents were educators and had high education expectations for him. Aaron lived up to those expectations. He was super smart and took great care to balance his academics and extracurricular activities. Other kids in the band were like him too, and weirdly and unexpectedly, they all began to influence me. I went from not caring and having no real plans for my future, to aspirations of attending college and playing in the marching band. I was beginning to love music, and this, coupled with my relationship with Mr. Ventress and Aaron, began to change me and give me space to be around other like-minded people.

Aaron and his parents lived around the corner from me in the better part of the neighborhood, so I often rode home with them after band practice. During these rides and while spending time at their home, I'd often hear Mr. Ventress and his wife ask Aaron about classes and other things. Listening to these conversations and those of Aaron and other students at school, I became inspired to do the same things. Though I had never considered it before, I decided then that I wanted to go to college, so I began applying myself and doing whatever it took to make that a reality, including studying and going to the library. People were shocked that I even knew where the library was, but I was determined! The principal of my high school, Dr. Johnson, had gone to Louisiana State University (LSU) and earned two degrees from there. I liked him, and he was always bragging about LSU. On what seemed like a daily basis, he'd make it a point to tell us how great LSU was, so I wanted to go there too. I remember telling everyone that I was going to LSU just like Dr. Johnson.

Though I had started turning things around academically, I still struggled. Between the band, track and field, and academics, I had to work to balance it all. By the time my senior year rolled around, I was well into the swing of things. I excelled in school, and my immediate family was supportive, showing up to student events and games to see me perform. On top of my usual schedule, I was also Senior Class President, which added some additional responsibilities. As a student who had completely turned things around, you would think my teachers would be happy and supportive. While most of my teachers were, I had one teacher who seemed to always have it out for me. I was doing well in her class, yet she still went out of her way to bring me down. On days I had to perform for the band or attend student events, and we'd have to leave early for games, she'd question whether or not I needed to go. She would actively voice those concerns to the administration and other students of the senior class. However, that was nothing compared to her telling me that she didn't think college was for me or that I'd even be admitted. Talk about a dream killer! More specifically, she didn't think I'd ever get accepted into LSU, and I suppose she was right in one way or another. Imagine that, a young, impressionable kid with ambitions of being the first person in his immediate family to go to college, being told you would never make it, so you shouldn't even try. Years later, I would return to my old high school and show that same teacher that I had not only graduated from college with a bachelor's degree but that I was also a candidate for a master's degree.

The look on her face… priceless!

I applied to LSU twice, but I was denied admission. Even though I had done everything I could do to improve my grades, my test scores and grade point average just weren't satisfactory. I did not relent. I was determined to go to college, so I also applied to other schools, including McNeese State University, Grambling State University, Bethune-Cookman College, and Southern University and A & M College.

As much as I hate to say it, the Predominantly White Institutions (PWIs) admissions process was much easier to navigate. When I applied for admission into the Historically Black Colleges and Universities (HBCUs), I never knew what was going on with the process. The PWIs that I had applied to provided timely communication. In most cases, they gave options on what I could do moving forward, including enrolling in a community college and then transferring once my academic status was more favorable. Honestly, any news was good news to me. Other than my great-aunt, Jackie, and my cousins, Quincy Jr., and Jeremy, I was technically the first person in my immediate family to go to college, so I was just happy to be going through the process. My high school band director, Mr. Ventress, and my All-Star band director, Mr. Carnell Knighten, were both alumni of Southern, so they thought it would be the perfect fit for me and encouraged me to consider it. I had been under Mr. Knighten's leadership for about two and a half years as a member of the Louisiana Leadership Institute All-Star Marching Band, a band comprised of the top high school musicians from across the state of Louisiana. We would compete across the country and were often referred to as the "baby Southern" because of our style and sound. The first time I had flown on an airplane was my senior year in high school with LLI. I also traveled to Florida and California with LLI – my first real vacations out of Louisiana. I loved being in LLI. It made perfect sense to attend Southern since Mr. Knighten was also an assistant band director at the college. Somewhere between Southern's High School Band Camp, going to Bayou Classic and being apart of a marching band that compares to them, I finalized my decision and began applying to Southern University and A&M College.

By the time the spring semester of my senior year rolled around, I had already applied to Southern. I submitted my Free Application for Federal Student Aid (FAFSA) by the January 1st deadline. I was new to all of this, but my high school guidance counselor, Ms. Charles, had been super helpful and walked me through the entire process. I was excited yet nervous. Everyone else had begun receiving letters of acceptance and scholarship offers, but Ms. Charles assured me that mine would be arriving soon.

CHAPTER 3

A Dream Deferred

"What happens to a dream deferred? Does it dry up like a raisin in
the sun? Or fester like a sore- And then run?"

– Langston Hughes
Lincoln University '29

Breaking the Curse

My high school graduation was here before I knew it. It had been a long four years, but I had finally made it. I would officially be the first person in my immediate family to not only graduate from high school but also go on to attend college. As I stood on the field waiting to hear my name called to walk across the stage and receive my diploma, the weight of what this moment represented brought me to tears. I had not yet received my acceptance letter into Southern, but I knew I was leaving Opelousas, and I would not be coming back.

Graduation day was filled with sadness and joyfulness, as my mom and sisters were there to embrace and support me. My cousin, Deveral, and friend, LaShandra, ran down to the field with two huge signs, cheering my name and cutting flips in celebration of my graduation. Looking around, the people I loved most were there, but my dad and his side of the family was missing. It was a sour note to an otherwise special occasion. I had sent them invitations and pictures that I could barely afford, yet neither my dad nor anyone on his side of the family had bothered to show up. In some ways, I knew they wouldn't come, and in another, I had hoped I was wrong. I was the first grandchild and nephew to graduate from high school on that side of the family, and in the back of my mind, I thought this would mean something. I don't know if I really could have expected anything more. I hadn't spoken to my dad since my sophomore year after he and I had gotten into a physical altercation. Plus, by this time I had become a little more vocal about my father and the role he played in my life; my father's side of the family didn't take too well to that. I was sad at the moment, but by this time, I had already started losing respect for him and them, so the sadness dissipated as quickly as it came. I spent that night and the weeks ahead celebrating with friends and making preparations to start college in the fall of '06.

You Must Not Know Where You Are

Because I was in the LLI All-Star band, I spent a lot of time in Baton Rouge, the organization's home base. One day while I was there, I decided to visit Southern's admissions office to check on the status of my application. To my surprise, somehow, my application had gotten lost, so they had no record of me applying. It was a good thing I had proof that I had applied, including the documents Ms. Charles had submitted and copies of the money order I had sent to cover my application fees. I was clueless about what I should do now, so I did what the admissions representative advised me to do, and I waited to see if my documents would turn up.

Honestly, not much changed until after my audition for the Southern's marching band. After the audition, Mr. Knighten asked if I had received my acceptance letter, and I expressed that I hadn't been accepted yet. An admissions counselor had told me that some of my documents were missing. The admissions counselor advised that I wait to see if the system would update, indicating that the papers had been received. Mr. Knighten was not at all surprised and said, "Hahaha! Son, you must not know where you are! You need to go and tell them you need this processed now." At first, I didn't know what to make of what he was saying or what he meant when he said, "You must not know where you are," but I soon learned! I went back to the admissions office that same day, and they still didn't have any updates. I went back to Mr. Knighten, and he reassured me he would have someone review my admission status.

Some time passed, and I still hadn't received my admissions letter. I had, however, received an invitation to Crab Week for band camp. Crab Week was make it or break it for freshmen band members. To earn the "S" on your chest and become an official member of the Human Jukebox Marching Band, you'd first have to make it through this week, and then the few weeks after when the full band was present, and finally the entire first semester. I was so confused. How could I be invited to band camp but not accepted into the university? Not receiving my acceptance into the university was beginning to impact everything, including my housing arrangements. I needed housing to attend band camp, but I couldn't get accommodation because I had not been accepted into the university.

However, Mr. Knighten was able to get the Housing Department to allow me to move in, and he continued to assure me that things would work out, so I began preparing to leave home for college. I had a list of things I needed, and when I expressed this to my mom, she suggested that I ask my paternal grandparents for help. They hadn't done much to help me up to this point, so the chances of helping me as I prepped for college were slim to none.

Like most high school seniors or newly minted 18-year-olds, I had started receiving credit card offers in the mail. My family never talked much about financial literacy, so I didn't know what to expect or what I should or should not do, so I took advantage of the offers and used those credit cards to purchase the things I needed for school. By the time it was time to leave, I was all set. I still hadn't gotten my acceptance letter, but I had everything else I needed. I was excited yet nervous about being on my way!

As a freshman, you could not have a car on campus, so my mom drove me down to Baton Rouge and helped me set up my room. The drive was bittersweet. My mom had never been the emotional type, and most times, you'd have to read her body language to know what she was feeling, but somehow my leaving to go away to college was changing all of that. We talked the entire trip there, and she shared how she was proud of me and how she just wanted me to do well. I was her baby boy, and she wanted me to know that she had my back no matter what.

Once we got to campus and started moving everything into the dorm, it became more real. My mom cried and gave me a little Black boy angel that I still keep near my bedside to this day. She told me to think of her whenever I looked at the angel. Every time I looked at it, I remembered why I was there and that completing college was much bigger than me. I was there for my family and everyone who would come after me. I couldn't help but think about how hard it must've been for my mom not to experience going to college because she was a young teenage mother. I often think about how life would have turned out for her.

> **"For a woman, it ain't easy tryin' to raise a man."**
> – Tupac

We had to report to band camp right away, so my mom went to Walmart for groceries and last-minute items and finished prepping my room while I had gone to the camp meeting. She stuck around for a little while before leaving to go back to Opelousas. I was used to being independent, so I didn't realize that she still needed to be there until I saw that other band members' parents were still there. I called her to come back, and she came and stayed a little while longer until the band director dismissed all of the parents and told them they were free to leave. There was a mix of nervousness and excitement in the air. Parents had been dismissed from our band camp meeting, so everything became more real when they left. All of us freshmen band members, or "crabs" as we were called in the band world, were standing around talking and laughing when we noticed the room getting silent and doors beginning to lock. "What the hell is going on?" I thought to myself as I looked around. The senior band members, who were also section leaders, began rolling up their sleeves and calling out sections, "Okay, where all the tuba players at?" I slowly started walking over to my respective section when someone yelled, "You walking over here, you should be running!" At this point, I began tripping over myself, chairs, and everything else as I made my way to my section. Southern's tuba section leader at the time, Brandon Griffin, had been my section leader in high school my freshman year, so I felt somewhat safe and guarded. The section leaders announced that we were to report for practice at 6 a.m., and the only specifics they gave us beyond this was that we should not show up wearing our high school band shirts, which many of us had been proudly wearing since we arrived, and we had better look alike.

Me and my high school friends Jarrett and Aaron, who had also decided to attend Southern, already had a hint of what to expect. Mr. Ventress, our high school band director and Aaron's dad, shared some things with us about his experience. Walking back to the dorms that night, one of my crab brothers shared that his brother had told him that we should all shave our heads bald before reporting for practice the next morning. Now I have a pretty good memory and comprehension skills, and they hadn't said anything about doing this, so I was not convinced. Plus, I figured Brandon would have told me this before dismissing us from our crab meeting.

Engrossed by the excitement of it all, Aaron, Jarrett, and I spent most of the night watching videos of Southern and other high school bands on Marching Sport. Marching Sport was a band forum with videos that connected musicians. I met many of my crab brothers and sisters on Marching Sport.

When midnight rolled around, I noticed some of the guys pulling clippers out so they could shave their heads. I still didn't think this was something we were required to do until I saw other crabs walking around with their heads already shaved, so I went to my room and started shaving my head too. Around 2 or 3 a.m., we finally went to sleep, only to be awakened by a loud noise. At this point, it was about 5 a.m.

I had slept on campus before for Southern's Summer High School Band Camp, but we also had chaperones, so this was my first official night sleeping in a dorm room as a soon to be college student. The noise got louder and closer to our suite. All I could hear was people banging on doors and yelling. Honestly, my first thought was that we were being pranked. Yet somehow, even though this thought crossed my mind, I never moved. By the time the noise made its way to our room, I had realized it was something else. Someone opened the door to our suite, and all I saw was a sea of band shirts and people yelling, "Y'all need to get up and put your band clothes on!" Looking at the clock, I could see that it was way before the time we were told to report for practice, so why were they waking us up so early?

Still half asleep, we made our way downstairs. Some of us were running and clumsily putting on clothes as we stumbled out the doors of the dorm. The sun hadn't even come out yet, so it was still dark. All we could see were the section leaders' cars parked in a straight row, with their headlights beaming. We stood there, even a little confused because we'd been woken up out of our sleep. Unsure of what to make of everything, our fatigue quickly turned into alertness as the section leaders read us our rights and gave orders on how things would work from here on out. Somewhere during their speech, a freshman strayed in.

I guess he hadn't gotten the memo because not only was he late, but he still had hair on his head; this is what they meant by "look alike." He stood there looking even more confused than the rest of us as the band leaders asked if he noticed anything different about himself compared to the rest of us crabs. He quickly caught on that it was his hair, but he refused to cut off instead of opting to go home. One down, and this was only the first day! As the weeks went on, many more would eventually fall off too. I continued to stay the course. At this point, the thought of quitting never crossed my mind, even on days we practiced nonstop in the hot sun, and all we heard was section leaders yelling orders. I was determined to be a part of the band, and I hoped to become a band director one day, so quitting was not an option.

Southern has a military-style band, so to say the camp was challenging would be an understatement. It was all about discipline, precision, and consistency. Every note, movement, and speech served a purpose. That first day of camp, they broke us up by sections, and we immediately began rehearsing marching styles and fundamentals. The day was long and seemed like it would never end. It was the longest I had ever practiced at one time, and this was only a precursor of things to come. Band camp lasted four grueling weeks. We practiced six days a week and would start as early as 7 a.m., break for lunch and dinner, and end whenever the band director decided he was ready to stop, which meant we could be practicing as late as midnight, only to wake up a few short hours later and do it all over again.

After being at band camp for a little over a month, I finally got my university conditional acceptance letter. The admissions counselor told me that I didn't have the requirements to be fully admitted, but an online test and remedial courses would allow me to enroll. Mr. Jackson, Southern's lead director of bands, made a few calls on my behalf and got the process started for my conditional acceptance. He was genuinely advocating for me, and I'm more than sure it was his support and guidance that made the difference.

C H A P T E R 4

Southern Bound

**"You have to do the research. If you don't know
something, then you ask the right people who do."**
– Spike Lee
Morehouse College '86

It was a couple of days before classes were set to begin, and I had received my conditional acceptance letter. I mean, I wasn't too much bothered by enrolling in remedial courses; I was just excited to be attending college. I shared with my crab brothers and sisters my situation, and they were helpful throughout this process; they wanted to see me succeed. At this point, I was willing to do any and everything to stay at the school.

I was what you might call a super student. I was excited about being in college, so I had purchased all kinds of Southern University paraphernalia – the backpack, hat, t-shirt, posters, you name it, and I had it. I was officially a student on the campus of Southern University and A&M College. I was excited! I loved to dress, so I already had my outfit planned for the first day. You couldn't tell me anything.

I was fresh! My excitement was quickly interrupted when I realized that the only thing I would be wearing was my band uniform. If you were a crab, your band uniform was a white t-shirt, grey sweatpants, and white tube socks. Who wanted to wear that on top of having a bald head? We stood out. Everywhere we went, people knew we were band crabs. They respected and protected us. Black college marching bands are gems of the campus. I had never considered quitting out of all the stuff we had gone through in band camp, but this was a bit much. And we were not allowed to do things that most newcomers look forward to, like going to parties and hanging out at the Student Union. In the end, I stuck it out because I liked being in the band, I liked the people I was around, and I enjoyed learning. Most importantly, everything that we had gone through would teach us lasting life lessons.

Expectations

That first day on campus, I experienced what some might call culture shock. I know, a Black student at an HBCU, culture-shocked seems surprising, lol. I had never seen so many Black people in my life. Yes, I graduated from a high school with Black and White students, but this was the first time I'd ever seen so many Black students and Black instructors simultaneously. It was nice to be attending class with people who looked like me. I just couldn't understand why there were so many. When I did see a White person, I'd be like, "Oh my God, there's a White person on campus." Looking around at all the Black and brown faces, I began to understand the purpose of HBCUs better and why they exist. None of my White teachers had ever pulled me to the side in high school and told me where I needed to improve. They never offered guidance and additional support when I needed it most. But here, it was different. My instructors not only set the expectation for me to excel, but they also put me in the best position to do it, in both subtle and grand ways.

Besides my instructors and the administrators on campus, I could feel the weight of expectations from my community too. Every day I went to class, I'd remember the conversations I had with people back home or with men at the barbershop off-campus who, after finding out my friends and I attended Southern and played in the band, would tell us, "College is the place to be for young Black men. We need y'all to hold us down." These expectations set the stage for excellence and helped me realize the enormity of this opportunity. Where I come from, not many Black men leave the hood, go off to college, and become successful.

After finally being admitted into the university, attending my first day of classes, I thought everything was taken care of. My high school guidance counselor had helped me complete my FAFSA well before the deadline. I was told by Southern's financial aid advisor that I had enough financial aid to cover the costs, so I didn't think much of it when I started getting emails from the university about an outstanding balance. I seriously thought that maybe the emails were an error and were being sent to the wrong student. I must have ignored those emails one time too many because the next thing I remember getting is a notice on my dorm room door telling me that if I didn't make a payment, I would be kicked out of school. Oh no! I had worked so hard to get here, and there was no way I was going back to Opelousas. I didn't know what to do, so I went to my band director and showed him the letter. He told me I didn't have financial aid and needed to contact the financial aid office to work out my account issues. But how was I going to find time to do this? Between classes and band practice, I had little time to do anything else, let alone stand in line for financial aid … because the lines were LONG! I expressed this to my band director and my Aunt Jackie, and they both shared that if I got kicked out of school, then neither band nor classes would be a concern. Me: "Touché, say no more."

I made my way to the financial aid office, where the lines were wrapped around the building. The process of dealing with the financial aid office was far worse than the admissions process. Sometimes I'd leave band practice at 10 or 11 p.m., and there'd still be a long line outside the building. My aunt would call or email on my behalf and never get a response, and a few times, I went only to have to leave and go back later so that I could make it to class and band practice on time. What I would later discover is that the processing system was a bit outdated. You'll learn more about my financial aid experience later in the book.

They didn't answer phones or respond to emails, and most of the staff were older people who were not good with technology, not very open to change, and many of them were very rude. It wasn't entirely their fault. A lot of HBCUs have many students like me who need more hands-on attention. Like many HBCUs, the university lacked funding that would allow them to purchase systems that would make this process more streamlined. The salaries they paid employees in these positions were below average – trust me, I know from experience. **KEEP READING. IT GET'S BETTER!**

After going back and forth, I was finally able to speak with someone and was told I was missing documents. It went from this to me needing to have the financial aid director contact the billing office, so I would not be evicted from the university and my dormitory. By the time everything was processed, I was told I didn't have enough financial aid to cover my expenses. What was I going to do now? Like most students who came from a background like mine, my family could not help me. Frustrated, I went to Mr. Jackson and told him everything, and he offered me a band scholarship to cover my balance; I gladly accepted. Mr. Jackson had been instrumental in my growth and success as a college student.

CHAPTER 5

Roots

**"What's in front of you is a whole world of
experiences beyond your imagination. Put
yourself, and your growth and development, first."**
– Phylicia Rashad
Howard University '70

Getting into school, taking the placement exam, and navigating my way through the financial aid process was challenging, but I was officially taking freshman seminar classes and learning about Southern University A&M College and other HBCUs. I was amazed to know that there had been no colleges for Black people to attend not many years ago. The more I thought about it, the more I realized that without Southern University, I would not be here. This realization made me appreciate my college experience even more. I knew Southern was the school for me and that it had been created to allow people like me to obtain a college degree. Knowing that Southern chose me made me deeply appreciative. I was excited and empowered to take what I was pursuing even more seriously. I had already broken the curse in my family by graduating from high school, but I was ready to take on this new challenge and write a different narrative that included a 4-year college degree. Being at Southern would help shape my career and strengthen education gaps in my family and community.

That first semester was exhilarating, with many ups and downs. Here I was, officially a young adult on my own for the first time, a student at Southern University A&M College and a member of one of the most renowned collegiate marching bands in the world. I still remember my first college band performance. It was an away game against Bethune-Cookman College in Florida. It was my first bus ride with the band, and it took us an entire day to get there. Once we got there, the upperclassmen began preparing us for the performance with intense intimidation, lol. They told us that if we messed up the performance, they would make sure the band director kicked us out of the band or "zipped" us as they would call it. No pressure! We were already nervous, so telling us this only terrified us and made us even more nervous. As we stepped into the stadium, we could see thousands of people in the stands screaming. They hadn't seen the band perform for over a year, so the excitement level was off the charts. At that moment, I thought about all the times I had stood in the stands watching Southern's marching band perform, and now here I was on the other side of that. People went crazy the minute the snare drummers rolled their beat and the drum major, Louis Broadway, came out high kicking with style. I was nervous and could feel the butterflies in my stomach as I looked up and saw crowds of people singing and dancing along with us. Until that moment, I hadn't understood what I was becoming a part of, but now I knew. By the time we left the field, all I could remember thinking was, "We just did our first performance! I'm going to be on Marching Sport and YouTube where people are going to see me." That night we went back to the hotel and watched the show on Marching Sport. I called my mom and told her to look it up. She was just as excited as I was! That weekend was officially the beginning of my college experience. Every week after that was filled with studying, practicing, traveling, and performing.

"Discipline is not a dirty word."
– Janice Bryant Howard
North Carolina A&T State University '86

The entire thing was a routine I had to get accustomed to. I struggled to find my rhythm. I was practicing with the band, traveling, and performing at football games, but I neglected my classes and studying. Sometimes I'd sleep in and not go anywhere until 3 p.m. when band practice started. By mid-terms, I had C's, D's, and F's, and as my professors told me, it was because I didn't go to class, I wasn't assertive, and I didn't participate. My mind was focused, but only on band, not on both band and academics. What they'd told us in freshman orientation, "Look to your left and right, somebody won't be here next semester, but it won't be because the university failed them," was proving to be true. There was so much to get into and to easily distract you. In college, no one can make you go to class or do your assignments. I had to figure it out and quick. I knew I had to turn it around, so I did just that. I managed to meet my academic advisors, find the resources, and by the end of the semester, I brought my grades up. I was proud of myself. I had slipped a little, but at my core, I knew why I was there. I knew that people were counting on me to do well. I already had a taste of what it felt like to fail. I was determined never to experience that again. I developed a plan, and I stuck to it. I could no longer do what I had been allowed to do in the past. I had to remember all the people I was representing and those who helped me get here. I didn't feel like I had room for error, so I became very strict on myself, and I buckled down.

That first semester was all about discovery. While I struggled to find my footing in the classroom, I was also beginning to find my voice and discover who I was as a young, growing adult. I liked to talk, but I was shy at the same time. In large groups, I'd be quiet, but in small groups, I'd run it. I'd been a part of student government in high school, so college was no different. At the advice of counselors and mentors, I quickly became active on campus. I joined the Men's Federation and Collegiate 100 Black Men, a mentoring program for male students, and Student Government Association as a Class Representative.

The expression of freedom through visuals is something that Southern taught me. I would see a variety of styles from the students on campus. I don't know what it was, but females from New Orleans had the best fashions to me. Everyone had their unique style and identity. I wanted to do something different, something that would make me stand out from the crowd, so I decided to compete in the Mr. Sophomore Pageant. Once people found out I was competing, they kept asking me what I would wear for the swimsuit scene. My cousin, LaQuisha, pumped my head up to wear a speedo, and what do you know, I did just that! When those doors opened up, I had so much baby oil all over my body, looking like a disco ball, people were screaming and snapping pictures like the paparazzi. I didn't win the pageant, and I ended up losing to my cousin, Terrance, but I gained so much more than wanting a crown and a title. I gained the confidence to be free and try new things. For the longest, I hated my body. As a kid, I was teased about physical features that I could not change. Let's just say this, I haven't changed those features, and they all love them now. The day after the pageant, people complimented me, and I became known as "Travis with the Speedo." That pageant experience was one of many things that would help shape my experience at Southern University.

The Classic

Many college students get to go home during Thanksgiving break, but not all of us. If you went to Southern or Grambling and were a member of the band, your Thanksgiving break would be spent on campus practicing for the annual Bayou Classic festivities. Bayou Classic is one of the oldest, most televised, and visited Black football college experiences held in New Orleans, Louisiana. Bayou Classic is like one big family reunion. It's a love and hate situation between two excellent schools. My freshman year, my mom drove down and prepared a full Thanksgiving spread for me and my suitemates. She stayed for a while and even came out to the practice field in the cold to watch us rehearse. She was excited! My mom had always been supportive, but now that I was in college, she had become more involved in my college experience. She had all of the SU Mom gear and wore it proudly. Hearing my mom brag about her "baby boy" being on national television, performing with the Human Jukebox Marching Band made my heart smile. It would bring back memories of when she and I would be sitting home watching the Bayou Classic half-time show from the comfort of our home.

Storms

After the first semester of my freshman year, things began to flow a little more easily. I was finally in the groove of things. My band director had often told us that the fall semester would always be the easiest because the demands of band required that you keep a balance, and the freedom of spring would bring its temptations, which often meant you'd slack off a little more. For me, this was true. I found myself doing much better academically in the fall. I had finished my first semester with a 2.7 grade point average, but most of my crab brothers and sisters had a 3.0 or better. I would measure my academic standards against theirs, so I knew I needed to do better, and I did. My freshman and sophomore years came and went. I excelled academically, marching in the band, and a leader in different clubs and organizations on campus. By the time my junior year rolled around, I had hit my stride and started to think about life after graduation. I wish I could say junior year came and went, and everytong was all good, but it wasn't. It brought a new set of storms. Fall 2008, it was hurricane season, and the entire campus was on alert. Hurricane Gustav would be landing at any moment. Roads had been closed, and curfews had been put in place, so anyone who hadn't gone home was expected to be in the dorms. With a storm coming, you'd think we'd take it a little more seriously. Instead, being the college students we were, many of us were in the back of campus having what we called a Hurricane Party. Hurricane Parties are something the students from New Orleans had introduced to the campus. It is a party you have while a hurricane is going on. I know it may sound crazy, but it's safe. I mean, you're not really IN the hurricane partying, lol. Here we were having a good time. The sky was super dark. You could see military tanks rolling onto campus and setting up shelters. Amid everything, my phone rang. My sister had been calling me to get me to talk to my father all day because the doctors didn't think he'd make it through the night. He had been asking for me and insisting, " I need to talk to my son." I knew he was sick, but I was unphased, so I refused to talk to him. We never had a relationship, so it wasn't much to talk about, from my perspective. It was sad, but I had no place in my heart for him.

Finally, I answered the phone. On the other end was my mom telling me my father had passed away. I didn't know how to take the information or whether I should be happy or sad. This was the man I had been named after, and even though I had never spent more than a few moments with him, I had inherited a lot of who I am from him. The way I dress, my sense of humor, my blunt nature, and even my athleticism and build were all traits I had inherited from my dad.

Hearing that he had died was especially hard considering everything else that had happened within that week. On campus, we had no electricity but were required to go to band practice in preparation for a game against Tennessee State University. On top of this, my mom and siblings had been affected by the storm too. It was a lot to take in, so that call from my mom completely caught me off guard.

Even though my father wasn't in my life, I knew he was alive, and I knew who he was to me. Going through all of this and trying to figure out college life was stressful. As I hung up with my mom, the police came in and started directing everyone to leave. I remember smashing my phone to the ground and running off. The lights were flashing, and the police were coming down on motorcycles and four-wheelers as I ran through the field. I made it to the security checkpoint and was greeted by guards standing there with guns drawn. They instructed me to stop where I was and to put my hands up. I stood there numb, unable to say anything. They asked for my name and my student I.D., and I just couldn't say anything. I was just there. The guards took me to the police station on campus and handcuffed me to a chair. I was the only person who had been arrested that night. Luckily, one of the ladies who worked there recognized me and asked me what I was doing there. I just stared. She continued to ask if I was okay, and eventually, the tears would start to roll down my face as the pain in my heart struck hard. She called out to the guards and told them that she knew me and that I was a student. By this time, they had started booking me and writing up charges because I had violated the curfew. Beginning to shake out of the daze I had been in, I started talking to the lady. As we spoke, I could hear people in the other room. It was my friends. Several people had seen the police arrest me, so they had come to the station looking for me. They told the officers that my father had just died. Between my friends and the lady who worked at the station, the officers decided to let me go. I did get a ticket that was later resolved, but they didn't file any charges.

When my father passed away, my older sister and I stopped talking for a couple of months. Unlike my dad and I, she and my dad always had a close relationship. In her mind, all he wanted to do was see and talk to me, so she couldn't understand why I had refused. She had my mom in her life, and she's the oldest grandchild for my dad's parents, so she always had them in her corner and didn't experience the rejection that my younger sister and I did. My dad lived with my grandparents, so she was more like his sister than his daughter because my grandparents took care of both of them. She had been there with him for doctor's appointments and making sure he took his medications. She was always by his side. In the end, we put our differences behind us, and that was the start of building a stable sibling relationship. P.S. I have the best big sister ever! Love you, Nik Dog!

C H A P T E R 6

I Think So, But I'm Not Sure

**"If you feel like there's something out there that
you're supposed to be doing if you have a passion
for it, then stop wishing and just do it."**
– Wanda Sykes
Hampton University '86

For as long as I can remember, I wanted to be a band director. I would sometimes play my band music, put on a suit jacket and white gloves, and stand in the mirror pretending to conduct a band. I even kept a large binder of marching band drills that I had charted and knew for sure that my future band would perform them. No one told me to do these things; I was just that passionate and motivated. I had studied marching band for a long time and knew exactly what I wanted my band to look and sound like, but then something changed. Of course, I liked music, but did I like it enough to be a band director for the rest of my life? I had always wanted to go into education, starting from when I was younger. I'd admire my elementary school teacher, Mr. Murphy. Mr. Murphy was a great mentor and teacher.

He created an organization, "Young Men of Promise," to promote positivity in young male students like myself. Mr. Murphy would even host Bible study meettings for us. This was probably one of the first "safe spaces" I had as a young kid. But somehow the idea of being an educator changed. I love music and everything that it offers. Th e dream of being a band director had traveled with me from Opelousas to Baton Rouge and was a massive part of the reason I was at Southern. Hence, the decision to pivot from education entirely was not easy.

I began reflecting on the conversations I had with Mr. Knighten as far back as my senior year in high school. At the time, I didn't want to hear it, but Mr. Knighten had insisted that the only reason I wanted to be a band director was because of him and Mr. Ventress. I didn't express it then, but I was crushed. Back then, I really couldn't imagine myself doing anything else, but now I was questioning whether he had been right all along. Reluctantly, I went to his office and told him that Music Education just wasn't working out and that I was thinking about changing my major. He pulled an "I told you so" and told me that I should give mass communication a shot. It took some convincing, but the more I thought about it, the more it made sense. That same semester I changed my major from Music Education to Mass Communication. I hadn't even considered any for the change, but lucky for me, there were none. I had changed my major at the top of my junior year, so all my credits would count towards my new program.

The transition to my new major was weird. I was surrounded by people who spoke exceptionally well, and it was a bit intimidating. I didn't know anything about how you should talk as a reporter, being on camera, knowing your angles, or anything for that matter, so it took some time to learn and adjust. But as time passed, I had begun to love the new program. I met JJ, Charisse, Brittany, and Jessica in the program. They were all accommodating and would become great friends after college.

One of the first classes I took was Communication Law. The professor who taught the class was about 6'2, and she would wear outfits that matched from head to toe. If she wore a black leather jacket, you better know she'd also have on a black leather skirt, a black leather shirt, and a matching black leather hat. Being at an HBCU, I shouldn't have been surprised because almost everyone had a great sense of style and fashion. That first day in class, she went down the roster and asked everyone about their classification. When she got to my name, she knew right away that I was new, so she said, "Oh, you're new to the program, and you're taking Com Law. Well, good luck to you because I see a lot of repeat offenders in here." This was the class that would make or break you as a mass communication student. As I got to know other students in the class, I soon learned that some took this class three and four times. In the back of my mind, I thought it couldn't be that hard. The class required you to learn all the laws about mass communication alongside Southern's law school students, one of the nation's top HBCU law schools. As tough as it was, everything worked out, and I ended up earning a B in the class.

Although I was loving the Mass Communication Department, I missed being in the music department. Everyone from the marching band had seemed to be music majors. I had gone from seeing them every day, in almost every class, to rarely seeing them on campus during the day. I still managed to incorporate marching band into my project assignments. I would record videos and news stories for the department. The following summer, I did a short-lived internship at WAFB news station. They had student interns from all over, including Southeastern Louisiana University and LSU, but their bias against Southern students was blatant. We were all young and eager to learn and get more experience, but that didn't seem to matter. There was no fairness system, and it was evident that students from Black schools were treated differently. Students from White schools got most of the hands-on and in front of camera experience. Those of us from Black schools were forced to play in the background. I don't remember how long I stayed, but I eventually quit because I felt it was a waste of time.

The same summer, I landed another internship, this time, it was at Southern's news station. I wish I could say it was better, but it wasn't for entirely different reasons. While the department professors were outstanding, there was only so much they could do with limited resources. The interns were doing more part-time administrative tasks. This is one area that I felt we could have used improvement. Although we did have professors like Dr. Bickham and Dr. Campbell who made sure we were still learning the material and getting the best experience.

CHAPTER 7

Welcome To The Real World

"Anytime you see a turtle up on a top of a fence post, you know he had some help."
– Alex Haley
Elizabeth State Teachers College

By senior year, I was like Mr. All American; I was that dude. I was still fairly active on campus and held leadership positions in different organizations. By this point, I just knew I was about to graduate and get a job making $100k. A lot had changed. I was more mature and not the same small-town boy who had come to Southern's campus just three short years ago. I had a world view that I didn't have my freshman year, and I knew how to communicate effectively amongst my peers. I knew I still needed to get some things together, but I was confident in the path I wanted to take. I made things happen, surrounded myself with the right people, and geared up to take those next steps into the real world.

As I looked back, I reflected on the people I had started with, some of them would be walking across that stage too, and others had either dropped out along the way or would be staying a little while longer to finish out this leg of their journey.

Graduation Day

I got no sleep the day before graduation. We had a rehearsal that Thursday, and immediately afterward, I went back to my apartment with my cousin, Ryan Keith, who was also graduating. We spent the night reminiscing about our time at Southern. We were both first-generation college students, a fact that was not lost on either of us. We knew what this moment meant! Graduation is a big deal, especially at an HBCU where you may be the first person in your family to graduate from college. We spent the entire night talking, and periodically friends would pop up with cards and gifts. Some of them were even asking for advice, but I didn't know what to say other than staying the course and finishing.

The day of graduation, lack of sleep, and staying up all night talking caught up with me. I was literally in graduation, trying hard not to doze off. As I looked around the room, I could almost name all of the people I was graduating with. Our paths had crossed at some point or another, and now here we were, entering the real world as graduates of Southern University and A&M College. Everything about this moment was unforgettable! As they called my name, I walked across the stage, and I knew this was it. I had broken the hedge and established a new reality for my family. Now my youngest sister, nieces and nephews could chart a different course for their lives.

As I exited the stage, the band members there cheered me on. I searched the crowd and spotted my mom. There she was, happy and proud, crying. Her baby boy had graduated from college. Though we weren't wealthy by any stretch of the imagination, my mom had made many sacrifices to get me to this place, and I was grateful. My sisters, godmother, and my aunt, my dad's sister, were there too. They had been my biggest supporters, and here they were cheering me on, on my big day. This was the best day of my life!

The Job Market

While I hoped I would land a six-figure job right out of college, it just didn't happen. Before graduating, I had applied for plenty of jobs, but no one tells you that even with a degree in hand, a down economy could affect your job search. When it wasn't the economy, it was just plain old discrimination. I remember seeing job posts for companies that only accepted LSU graduates as if there wasn't another university with equally qualified graduates just down the road. Granted, maybe those companies were owned by LSU graduates, but this is why we need more HBCU graduates in positions of authority. Not to show favoritism, but so there is a pipeline.

I graduated in May 2010, right after the Great Recession, which was rough. I couldn't get a job anywhere – no news companies or some other company as a P.R. specialist. I couldn't even get a job at Walmart. I applied for hundreds of jobs before finally landing my first job fresh out of college at Taco Bell. Yes, I had a degree working at Taco Bell. While some people would have been embarrassed, I wasn't. I knew where I came from, and I had always seen my mom grind and get it, so it never struck me that, "Hey, you have a degree, and you're working at Taco Bell." Plus, I just really needed a job, and I knew where my next meal was coming from, literally. I had roommates, and I needed to keep up with my portion of the rent. The manager who hired me, Brad, knew I had a college degree and that I wouldn't be there long, so he encouraged me to learn whatever I could, take it, and move on.

I worked at Taco Bell for almost a year before I got my first official job in my career field, working as a P.R. Specialist for a local furniture store. I wrote all the scripts for their commercials, newspaper writeups and laid out its sales ad. At some point, they lost an account manager and needed someone to take over the position. I guess they figured because

I had a college degree, I could do it. I was hesitant and told them accounting wasn't my thing, but I agreed after a little nudging. Surprisingly I was excellent at it. This would be my first experience with finance and audits – little did I know it would come in handy. I was making a bit more money; I had benefits and some weekends off. I was becoming more stable and moving in the right direction.

My former college band director, Mr. Jackson, would periodically call to check on me to see how things were going. One day he called, and I told him about my experience trying to find a job and that the job I currently had allowed me to use my degree, but I was only making $28k. He responded, "Oh, Opelousas, $28k? That's not enough money for you?" He told me that he might have something for me and that he'd call me back.

He called a couple of days later and told me there was a recruiter position open at the university. I applied, interviewed, and was offered the job. Something happened with a change in leadership in the Office of Admissions and Recruitment, and things were taking longer than expected to start. Then, a position became vacant in the Office of Financial Aid. Even though I had graduated, I was still helping out with the band. I was the person guiding freshmen band members through the pipeline of financial aid because

I had been through the process and knew what was required, so this new position seemed like a better fit. I asked Mr. Jackson what he thought about me going into financial aid instead, and he thought it would be perfect. I think he liked the idea of having someone to assist him with band members paying for school and navigating the financial aid process, while he focused on putting a band together. I can't blame him. Now let's pause right here... I just couldn't believe I was considering working in financial aid. Eight years later, me to me: "I wish the university had a Travis working in financial aid while I was in school and marching in the band."

The position in financial aid paid more, plus I wouldn't have to travel. I applied, and I got the job. I officially started in July of 2012. When I got there, they knew I had been doing P.R. work, so they had me on projects to redesign the website, forms and enhance the communications sent to students and parents. I was enjoying working here, and I loved interacting with students and parents.

When I first started working on campus, I felt like an employee but still a student. I had just graduated from Southern two years prior, so I knew most students there. People were saying things like, "Oh, Travis didn't graduate," or they'd say I was visiting the campus too much, lol. A lot of people didn't realize I'd gotten a job working for the university.

Being on campus again felt like home. I would sometimes go to the student union and just look at the students, and it would take me back to my memories of being a student on campus. The way they danced, laughed, and the things they talked about seemed far too familiar.

Every day driving across the hump, especially as the sun was setting right behind the water on what we call the Bluff, and all you could see was the Columbia blue and gold flags, I'd think to myself, "This was the place that gave me everything I needed to become the person that I am today." I was back as an employee, but for me, I needed to give the students my all because I owed them the same service and gratitude I either had or didn't have as an undergraduate. I also wanted to be the change that I wanted to see. I had experienced some unpleasant things during my time at the university. Remember, in Chapter 4 I wrote, "Keep reading. It gets better?" I would later find out that low pay, being short-staffed, and not having many resources would contribute to unhappy staff and low morale. They were doing the best with what they had, and because I had seen and experienced so much of it firsthand, I knew I could come in and make a real difference. I had a fresh set of eyes and ears and had at one time been on the other side.

Some people think that working in financial aid is just

sitting behind a desk processing paperwork and answering phones, but for me, it's bigger than that. Being able to afford school is essential. Without the ability to finance school, students either do not attend college or struggle to make payments. After being admitted into the university, the next thing is the financial side of it. Everything else comes after that. You can be the most brilliant student with a 4.0, but if the finances aren't in order, it's not going to happen for you. So that was my task, to make the financial aid process as seamless as possible for parents and students. They'd come into my office, and I'd instantly be taken back to my time as a student entering the financial aid office and being clueless about why I was there. I caught on to financial aid quickly. It took me three months to grasp the basics of my role.

By September, I was processing and servicing students and doing many things that more seasoned financial aid advisors had been doing. I didn't know I would fall into financial aid of all places, but Sean, one of the guys who worked in the office, who later became a mentor and great friend, took notice and said that I looked like I was enjoying what I was doing. And I was. I love helping students, and they appreciate and respect me. I like to know that I am making a difference in the lives of college students and families.

When you work in student services at a university, you

are more than just your job description. Often what you say and do can be the difference between a student staying or leaving. While working at Southern, parents would compliment me and tell me how I made the process so much easier. I was extremely detailed and to the point. Students enjoyed my presentations. I was great at my job, and for the first time, I started thinking more seriously about pursuing a master's degree so that I could move up the ladder in higher education.

Sean was a great mentor. He had gotten both his bachelor's and master's from LSU. I liked the way Sean carried himself. He hadn't gone to an HBCU, but after working at Southern, he confided that one of his biggest regrets was not attending one. Sean's mother graduated from Grambling College; Grambling College was later named Grambling State University. Working at Southern made me fall in love with higher education. I was seriously thinking about all of the things I could do in higher education with a master's degree. At the time, I knew I didn't want to go to LSU, so I started looking at master's programs at Southern. That following fall, I enrolled in the Master of Public Administration program, hoping that I would be able to work on the federal level one day and help create and improve the rules and regulations that impact HBCUs' everyday lives.

Once I got into the MPA program at Southern, I started

to learn more about policies. There was one professor, Dr. Leslie Grover, who became a mentor to me. She was a "down-to-earth" professor, meaning she taught you by the book and gave you real-life experiences. She got me through graduate school and gave me the insight I needed to make it to the other side. One of the classes I took with her was a non-profit organization. In this class, every group was responsible for partnering with a non-profit organization and doing service work with them for the entire semester. My group partnered with the National Alliance on Mental Illness (NAMI) and even helped set up a chapter of the organization on campus for our final project.

Graduate school is where I met friends from other HBCUs. Some of them had come from Grambling, Alabama State University, and Tuskegee University. We would have conversations and discover that we had many shared experiences. While most of us had attended HBCUs in undergrad and then continued that trend for graduate school, some students had started graduate school at PWIs. Many of them had transferred to Southern because the PWIs didn't give one-on-one attention, and in most cases, made them feel like they were just another number. This was the beauty of HBCUs, that feeling of community and belonging and one-on-one attention to nurture your growth and development. It is this level of nurturing that sharpened us and readied us for the real world.

New Horizons

Mr. Jackson set the foundation for the type of leader I wanted to be, but Ursula Shorty, Director of Financial Aid, set the tone for the type of administrator I would later become in higher education. She was everything that I envisioned someone's boss or supervisor in the workplace to be. She did excellent training, her communication was good, and she inspired you to be great. She would always tell us, "I don't train people to be mediocre. I train directors." I later found this to be accurate because three of my former coworkers, under the direction of Ms. Shorty, became directors.

As the years went on and I noticed the impact I was having on students and their parents, my perspective began to change. Graduation was getting closer, and though I hadn't told anyone, I had already started applying for jobs in other places. I loved working at Southern, but I needed to grow more; I needed to go out and see how other schools were operating. In January of 2016, I received a call from Texas Southern University (TSU). TSU is one of the largest HBCUs located in the heart of Houston, TX. It had been so long since I applied for a job there that I didn't remember. Within one phone call, I was offered the job. It was $15,000 more than what I was making at Southern, so I accepted.

At the time, TSU was going through a reorganization process. As part of that restructure, they were creating a customer service division that would assist with students' and parents' complaints and delays in processes. They increased staffing, so my area within the financial aid department was a new addition. I was excited! They never had it before, so whatever I put into place would be the start of laying the foundation.

The transition to TSU was great. I was little old Travis from a small town, moving to Houston and working in higher education. I was moving up the ladder in financial aid and administration. Working at TSU was cool because I didn't know anyone on campus, so I could make a name for myself without anyone pulling on me because they knew me as "T.J. from the band."

On the second day on the job, I got a visit from students on the Student Government Association. I had seen one of them before, but I couldn't place how I knew him. He walked in and immediately called me by name. I was still confused about how he could know me because I didn't know any students. I soon discovered his name was Justin Lee, and he had gone to Central High School in Beaumont. Justin came to Southern's band camp a few summers when I was a section leader.

It was a full-circle moment. Justin had found out about me through an HBCU SGA group chat. The Southern students had told them I would be coming to work at TSU, and they should get me to help. Not tooting my own horn, but I did put together some good threads (clothes), and I did a great job working with the students. Justin had come into the office with Miss TSU, Cassandra Canute. They were the first two students I met at the university; it meant a lot that they didn't know me, yet they were looking for me to be their campus advisor.

While working at TSU in financial aid and being the Royal Court Advisor, I learned that the students were much like Southern students. They were talented and ambitious students. I quickly became the mentor I had in my early college years. It is essential to have a mentor in and out of the classroom, someone you will learn from, and not afraid to tell you when you are wrong. My best mentors came from Southern. I wanted to be to the students what Mr. Jackson was to me. Both the students at SU and TSU helped me become a better person and redefine passion. Because of them, I continue to create avenues for students to have representation at the table. I am always inspired by stories of victory, triumph, and success. Often, our students need us as that extra boost to get them across the finish line.

I worked at TSU for two years before leaving to accept a campus director position at a community college, one of the nation's largest community college systems. They were excited to interview me, and I was excited to be interviewing for them. I mean, here I was, out here accomplishing goals one step at a time. The interview committee went through my background and was thoroughly impressed with my resume and personal experience. You have to remember, I was far from the smartest person in my K-12 classes and struggled a bit in college. They hired me on the spot and asked if I could start within a week. I was excited, but there was no way I could begin that soon without giving TSU notice.

Unlike other schools I'd worked at, this community college had more resources and structure. With eleven different campuses, one campus might have been predominantly White, another Hispanic, one more mixed, and then another reflective of what you might see at an HBCU. Interestingly, it was mostly an adult or non-traditional student population. The campus I worked at was primarily Black. Overall it was a good experience. The students had similar backgrounds, and because of my experience, I could relate to them.

I eventually left the community college to work at another HBCU. This HBCU is a private university; for conversation purposes, we'll call this school HBCU X. HBCU X was a lot different than all of the colleges I had worked for. Their systems and processes were more antiquated, but unlike the other schools I'd worked at, they had more aid to offer students. This was a unique situation because the students were much like SU and TSU, but middle leadership was slightly different. The university president was phenomenal and searched for building a team that could take HBCU X to the next phase.

Anything you could think of, they would provide. You could call with a ridiculous request for ten Mac computers and 50 flat-screen T.V.s. They would order it and have it delivered by the end of the week with no problems, whereas at other HBCUs I'd worked at, you could ask to order some sticky pads, and there would be this long-drawn-out process and discussion before the purchase would even be considered. Working at HBCU X allowed me to see how having the right resources and leaders can take a school to the next level. HBCU X also recruited many students from New Orleans, so I sometimes encountered students who knew some of the same people I knew, or in some cases, I had advised their siblings at SU or TSU. I wasn't at HBUC X long, but I was able to help change a lot of things about their systems and processes in the short time I was there.

CHAPTER 8

The Future Of HBCUs

"Education is the key to move mountains, to build
bridges, to change the world."
– Oprah Winfrey
Tennessee State University '86

I have a long way to go, but I'm proud of what I've been able to accomplish. I must continue the advocacy for all HBCUs. My HBCU gave me hope, vision, and an opportunity. You see, when you come from the trailer park and the hood, people judge you before they get a chance to hear your story. Southern University and A&M College allowed me to tell my story. Not only did I tell it, but they listened and responded. When you struggle academically your entire life, the last place you think you'd make a career is in education. I guess for me, it was different. The reason that I am here is because of my struggle. I know what it's like to be called a failure before you're allowed even to try. I know what it's like to be labeled because of your background. I know what it feels like to be looked down on because I sing the tune for those who don't have a stage to sing. When some people see a young Black man with tattoos pursuing a doctorate with aspirations of becoming a university president, it baffles them. From that perspective, I feel I've had to go ten times harder because they aren't used to seeing people like me in these roles. I am often reminded that I represent many people. We don't pick our upbringings and challenges as kids, and we shouldn't let that determine our future.

Never in a million years did I ever think I'd be doing what I'm doing now. And this is only the beginning! I'm currently pursuing a doctorate so that one day my dream of leading HBCU initiatives, policies, and reforms become a reality. I realize that the only reason this dream is possible is because of Southern University and A&M College. They took a young, immature, and ignorant kid from Opelousas and nurtured him to success and promise. Whatever your story is, I'm confident the same can be done for you. Even if you aren't the best student, you too can rewrite your story, change your habits and get on the right path, one that hopefully leads you to *Apply HBCU!*

I think we often forget, but it's important to remember why HBCUs were created. The reality is that HBCUs were made because, at one time, there was no space for Blacks to attend college and acquire higher education. We must remember what the founders of HBCUs fought for. Our communities are filled with underserved and impoverished students, and it is essential that they, too, understand there is a space for them, much like Southern was for me. While every student that attends an HBCU is not like me, and some come from wealthy and two-parent, educated households, many don't.

At an HBCU, you are afforded an education and degree similar to a degree from any other school. For many of us, just being afforded an opportunity as a low-income individual is nothing short of remarkable. You ask any graduate of an HBCU, and they'll likely tell you the same thing. My HBCU is where I was educated and cultivated to become the person I am today. It's also where I met the family – people who looked like me and shared similar stories and experiences. At an HBCU, you can fully be yourself as you learn from one another. You also have those aunts, uncles, mother, and father, and in some cases grandparent figures, around campus that care about your well-being and make sure you're good.

I've had mentors around campus purchase books for me or tickets to go on trips. They had a vested interest in my success and wanted to make sure I got the full college experience. Mr. Jackson helped bring out the best in me. He taught me that with hard work, networking, dedication, and education, I could go a long way. He also taught me always to stay the course, and if nothing else, to be fair and neutral. And this is the HBCU experience. My goal is to one day be the president of an HBCU with a team of innovative change agents who have a passion for servicing students and uniting alumni. I envision a time when all HBCUs will soar with enrollment increases and high graduation rates. A time when all alumni are on one accord holding not only university administration accountable but local, state, and federal leaders responsible for fair treatment of funding and resources; and welcome our fellow alumni to high standards of being involved. I envision leading an HBCU with my Triple Cs' philosophy – Comfortable, Committed, and Confident. Both alumni and administration must be comfortable to talk about the challenges we see with our schools. We must be committed to having those conversations, and we must be confident in finding a resolution. HBCUs are necessary and will always be necessary. So if you look like me and think your existence isn't purposeful, remember our ancestors and HBCU founders did not stand up so we can give up. Your presence matters somewhere, and for many, the discovery of this fact begins at the open doors of an HBCU. I encourage you to Apply HBCU and discover the very thing that I and countless others before you have discovered…

HBCU Experiences

"Southern University provided the unyielding support and unique environment I desperately needed. My professors and the administrators met my needs because many of them understood where I came from. An HBCU experience, to me, is a rite of passage that I was privileged to experience before starting my adult life as a "minority" in America."

Siedah Robinson
Southern University and A&M College, 2011
B.S. Accounting

"HBCUs are one of the few, if not only, times in your life where you can be completely immersed in Black Excellence every day. They are rich in history, bring together the best and the brightest, and preview the future and if we can come together as one. Black is beautiful, and HBCUs are brilliance personified."

Ray B. Shackelford
Morehouse College, 2008
B. A Business Administration/Finance

"For me, attending an HBCU meant legacy, safe haven, and pure intellectual curiosity. I was fortunate to have been the result of three generations of an HBCU education. For the first time in my travels through America, could I truly have my wit evaluated through no optical view of race? The legacy has given me purpose, responsibility, and most of all courage to seek the dreams I wish for and to B.E. the change I want to see."

Jarred C. Morgan
Florida A&M University, 2003-2008
B.S. Accounting/Finance
FAMU and Shanghai University
Masters of Business Administration

"Attending an HBCU means opportunity, self-realization, cultural pride, and ownership. The experience provided a sense of freedom that I wasn't aware existed or felt I was missing. It was the best decision I ever made!"

Tiffany Hughes
Grambling State University, 2008
B.S. Early Childhood Education

"Alcorn State University is simply the best thing to ever happen to me, thus far, in my adult life. I learned so much; I had so much fun! Now, as an alumnus, there is still so much to experience."

GeColby Youngblood
Alcorn State University, 2010
B.A. English Literature

"Attending an HBCU for all of my degrees gave me a sense of determination. Studying at an institution along with scholars that looked like me made me feel accepted and supported. My HBCU's provided the foundation I needed to excel in my field, and they continue to inspire others to do the same."

Henry J. Henderson III
Southern University and A&M College, 2013, B.S.
Tuskegee University, 2015, M.S.
Tuskegee University, 2019, Ph.D.

"Historically Black colleges and universities have been the root of Black success and excellence in America. My HBCU experience has afforded me a quality education and a platform to mentor young kids who look like me. HBCUs cultivate Black students for a better tomorrow."

Ramon Jackson
Jackson State University, 2014
B. A. Music Education Jackson State University,
2016 Masters of Music Education

"I had the pleasure of becoming a 4th generation graduate of THE Fort Valley State University where I met the love of my life, Jasmine. Attending an HBCU was the best decision I ever made because I wasn't taught WHAT to learn, but HOW to learn. This has served me when learning HOW to be a good husband, father, professional, mentor, and the list goes on. Prayerfully my namesake will follow in our footsteps and attend an HBCU so that he can be as proud of his heritage as Fort Valley State University taught his parents to be."

Cody Langston Sr., MBA
Fort Valley State University, 2009
B.S. Agricultural/Plant Science

"As a proud engineering graduate of Southern University and A & M College, the HBCU experience is like no other. I was cultivated in a rich culture that built confidence and prepared me with the essentials to be successful in life and take those acquired skills back to my community in hopes to uplift and build others that look like me. There is just something about that HBCU pride."

D'Tara Frank
Southern University and A&M College, 2011
B. S. Civil Engineering

"For me, attending Morehouse was one of the most formative experiences of my life. Most people would have been turned off by the rigor of dealing with the front office, the antiquated facilities, and the costly tuition. However, to me, all these "obstacles" only helped to shape my character as a Black man in America; and birth an insatiable thirst for greatness."

Christopher M. B. Jones Morehouse College, 2009
B.A. in History

Resources & Tips

Applying for an HBCU

After you apply, follow-up. Most schools will send out confirmation communication, but you will have to follow-up when you get into the real world, so go ahead and put that habit into practice.

Meet all deadlines. This includes deadlines for admissions, financial aid, housing, and any special programs critical to your degree program. If possible, apply early. Keep track of everything by creating a spreadsheet with four separate rows listing:

- The task to be completed

- The deadline to complete the task

- The date the task was completed; and

- Follow-up/Confirmation (if necessary)

Keep good records. If there is a mix-up or a document is lost in the shuffle, you can easily access missing documents and resubmit them right away. Create an "important folder" in your email.

Don't make assumptions. If you don't understand, don't be afraid to ask questions. There is always someone there to assist you. If you're not sure who that is, ask.

Attending An HBCU

You're young, you're growing, and you're learning. Being around so many different types of people from different walks of life can be overwhelming. Surround yourself with people who will motivate and inspire you to follow the path of the vision you have for your life. You'll make mistakes, but make sure you have the right mentors who can help you navigate these things.

Become an active part of the campus. Sometimes you hear people complain about their experience at an HBCU, but it's usually because they are disconnected. The thing that makes HBCUs so different and unique is the culture and community, so take advantage of that. HBCUs were created for us, so everything they do is for you. At HBCUs, students have a voice in helping to shape the campus's vision, so get involved.

United Negro College Fund (UNCF)- www.uncf.org

In addition to offering scholarships, they also have local counselors to assist you in navigating the admissions process and figuring out what HBCU is the best fit for you and your goals.

Common Black College App-

www.commonblackcollegeapp.com

Apply to more than 50 HBCUs with one application, and pay only one fee.

Federal Application for Student Aid (FAFSA)-

www.fafsa.gov

Apply for financial assistance, including grants and loans.

Alumni Chapters – Find an alumni association of the school you want to attend and connect with them for resources and information.

Historically Black Colleges & Universities

Alabama A&M University

Alabama State University

Albany State University

Alcorn State University

Allen University

American Baptist College

University of Arkansas at Pine Bluff

Arkansas Baptist College

Barber-Scotia College**

Benedict College

Bennett College

Bethune-Cookman University

Birmingham-Easonian Baptist Bible College*

Bishop State Community College

Bluefield State College

Bowie State University

Carver College *

Central State University

Charles Drew University of Medicine and Science *

Cheyney University of Pennsylvania

Claflin University

Clark Atlanta University

Clinton College

Coahoma Community College

Concordia College, Alabama (closed 2018)

Coppin State University

Delaware State University

Denmark Technical College

Dillard University

University of the District of Columbia

Edward Waters College

Elizabeth City State University

Fayetteville State University

Fisk University

Florida A&M University

Florida Memorial University

Fort Valley State University

Apply HBCU

Gadsden State Community College (Valley Street campus)

Grambling State University

Hampton University

Harris-Stowe State University

Hinds Community College at Utica

Hood Theological *

Howard University

Huston-Tillotson University

Interdenominational Theological Center

J. F. Drake State Technical College

Jackson State University

Jarvis Christian College

Johnson C. Smith University

Johnson C Smith Theological Seminary *

Kentucky State University

Knoxville College **

Lane College

Langston University

Lawson State Community College

LeMoyne-Owen College

Lewis College of Business (closed 2013)

The Lincoln University

Lincoln University

Livingstone College

University of Maryland Eastern Shore

Meharry Medical College

Miles College

Miles School of Law *

Mississippi Valley State University

Morehouse College

Morehouse School of Medicine

Morgan State University

Morris Brown College

Morris College

Norfolk State University

North Carolina A&T State University

North Carolina Central University

Oakwood University

Paine College

Paul Quinn College

Payne Theological *

Philander Smith College

Prairie View A&M University

Rust College

Saint Paul's College (closed 2013)

Savannah State University

Selma University

Shaw University

Shelton State Community College- C A Fredd Campus

Shorter College

Simmons College of Kentucky

South Carolina State University

Southern University at New Orleans

Southern University at Shreveport

Southern University and A&M College

Southwestern Christian College

Spelman College

St. Augustine's University

St. Philip's College

Stillman College

Talladega College

Tennessee State University

Texas College

Texas Southern University

Tougaloo College

H. Councill Trenholm State Community College

Tuskegee University

University of the Virgin Islands

Virginia State University

Virginia Union University

Virginia University of Lynchburg

Voorhees College

West Virginia State University

Wilberforce University

Wiley College

Winston-Salem State University

Xavier University of Louisiana

Not recognized by U.S. Department of Education as an HBCU

** Not currently accredited **

Made in the USA
Middletown, DE
11 November 2021

52149054R00053